Freedom of

Movement

Catherine Bradley

FRANKLIN WATTS
LONDON•SYDNEY

Revised and updated 2004

Franklin Watts
96 Leonard Street,
London
EC2A 4XD

Franklin Watts Australia
44-51 Huntley Street,
Alexandria
NSW 2015

© Franklin Watts 1997, 2004

Editor: Helen Lanz
Series editor: Rachel Cooke
Art Director: Robert Walster
Designer: Simon Borrough
Picture research: Sue Mennell
Consultant: Dan Jones of Amnesty
International

A CIP catalogue record for this book
is available from the British Library.

ISBN 0 7496 5902 5

Dewey Classification 323.44

Printed in Malaysia

Acknowledgements

Case studies on: Cambodia, Rwanda,
Vietnam and Central America are
based on examples from *State of the
World's Refugees* (UNHCR); China
and Nigeria based on material
supplied by Amnesty International;
Tigre based on information from
African Migrations, Dr Hakim Adi,
Wayland, 1994.

Picture credits:

Cover and contents page: Magnum
(Dennis Stock)

Amnesty International (UK) 36t, 43;
Daneford Trust 41t (Daisy Dunkley-
Clark); Hulton Getty Collection 8l,
15l; Hutchison Library 6bl (Crispin
Hughes), 11b, 13t, 30; (Robert
Francis), 38b, 40b; Image Bank 6br,
15r; Magnum Photos 23t (Eli Reed);
Panos Pictures 5 (Heidi Bradner), 6t
(Sean Sprague) 11m (Jim Holmes),
12b (Sean Sprague), 19r (Jon Spaull),
27 (Howard Davies), 28l (Howard
Davies), 39 (Borje Tobiasson), 42
(Anna Tully); Popperfoto 8r, 9, 11t,
17b, 19l, 20b, 21t (AFP), 21b, 29l &
r, 32b (AFP), 37t, 40tr; Raleigh
International 41b (Jonathan Topps);
Rex Features 16, 24, 25 (Sipa), 32t;
Frank Spooner/Gamma 10t, 17t, 20t,
22, 26t (Laski Diffusion), 26b, 38t;
Still Pictures 23b (Hartmut
Schwarzbach); Topham Picturepoint
7, 18, 28r (AP), 34, 36b, 37b (PA),
40tl; John Walmsley 12t; UNHCR,
Geneva 14tl & tr, 31 (E. Brissaud),
33t (H.J. Davies), 35 (A. Hollmann);
Zefa 10b.

The Publishers would like to thank
Daisy Dunkley-Clark and the
Daneford Trust for submitting their
photograph for use.

CONTENTS

If you go on holiday, have you ever thought about what your parents do before you go? If you are visiting another part of the country you live in, all they need to do is pack your bags and arrange to get there. If you are going abroad, you will probably need a passport. You may have to go to the embassy of the country you are going to visit to get a visa in your passport. A visa is a stamp that means that the embassy agrees to let you enter their country. It is not always easy to get a visa as the governments of some countries do not want visitors at all.

Visiting places of historical interest is just one reason why people travel overseas.

Tourism, or travelling to other countries for pleasure, is not only fun, but is also a way to learn a lot about how other people live. Going on holiday, however, is not the only reason people travel. Moving from one part of a country to another or travelling abroad means people can visit their families, do business or settle in different places. The opportunities to travel have led many people to leave home. Some 175 million people today live outside their country of birth – some have chosen this but others have been forced to leave their home – fleeing in order to survive.

As transport has improved, the world has 'grown smaller' as people are able to travel more easily. Business is now conducted between companies in different countries, as well as on the journey to visit the other company!

To travel abroad you usually need to take a passport so that officials at the border can check who you are.

'175 million people live outside their country of birth'

Freedom to move

Many people regard the freedom to leave home and to travel – their freedom of movement – as an important human right. In industrialized countries it is an expectation – a right often taken for granted. Some countries include it in their constitution – the statement on how the country should be run.

Restricting people's ability to move around is a loss of freedom. Someone who is prevented from travelling or is unable to choose where to live for no good reason is being denied his or her human rights.

What are human rights?

Human rights are those basic rights to which all human beings are entitled. They are based on the idea that everyone is equal and deserves fair and equal treatment. The idea of human rights has developed over the centuries. The Constitution of the United States of America, agreed in 1787, was one of the first significant examples of people's rights being included in the legal document stating how the country should be run. Since then, other governments have passed laws to uphold their country's idea of human rights.

Most people enjoy their freedom to go to whichever country they choose. They travel for pleasure – to get away from home and in order to relax and experience a different culture or climate.

Nations, an international organization to maintain world peace and security. The representatives agreed the United Nations Charter which was to prevent conflict, to respect equality and to protect fundamental human rights.

Representatives from the member states of the United Nations meet in New York.

Auschwitz, in Poland, was the largest and most infamous of the Nazi concentration camps. Here, 4 million people, mostly Jews, were worked or starved to death, or killed in the gas chambers as part of the Holocaust.

The abuse of human rights

Throughout history there have been many abuses of human rights. These range from people being killed because of their religion or because they were different, or being deprived of their freedom as slaves, to political opponents being tortured and imprisoned for their beliefs. In particular, during the 1930s and 1940s, Germany persecuted the Jewish people and set up concentration camps in which Jewish people were systematically killed. It is thought some six million European Jews died as a result of the Holocaust.

In June 1945, at the end of the Second World War, representatives from 48 countries from around the world met to establish the United

A common standard

In order to protect human rights, the United Nations adopted the Universal Declaration of Human Rights (UDHR) in 1948. The Declaration sets out the basic rights and freedoms that concern all aspects of people's lives from health and welfare, to rights concerning employment, political security and protection. It was designed to be 'a common standard of achievement for all peoples and all nations'. Several of its aims are specifically to protect freedom of movement and the rights associated with it.

Protecting freedom of movement

Freedom of movement is a right that belongs to every individual as well as whole communities. It refers to the right to move freely and safely within your own country and between countries. It includes the right to seek safety in another country if there is danger in your home country and it states that individuals should not be subjected to imprisonment or detainment without a lawful reason.

From the 16th to the 19th century, European traders shipped millions of Africans overseas to be sold into slavery, taking away their fundamental human rights including the freedom of movement.

Despite the efforts of the UDHR to protect people's freedom of movement, there are still people today who regard other people as their property and deny them basic rights. The slave trade was abolished by international treaty in 1885 and slavery was banned by the Slavery Convention in 1926. However, although no country officially supports it, slavery still exists in various forms in many parts of the world today.

Additionally, countries sometimes deprive citizens of the freedom of movement, if they believe these people represent a threat to others. Countries will imprison people who have used violence against others or who have destroyed properties, but sometimes people lose their freedom because they do not share the same political beliefs as the State, or because they have committed a small offence, such as not paying a fine.

This book looks at how the right to move freely has been affected by certain world events. It also looks at how successful the UDHR has been at protecting the freedom of movement.

These are some of the key articles of the Universal Declaration of Human Rights that are concerned with freedom of movement.

Article 3 Everyone has the right to life, liberty and security of person.

Article 4 No one shall be held in slavery or servitude; slavery and the slave trade shall be prohibited in all their forms.

Article 9 No one shall be subjected to arbitrary arrest, detention or exile.

Article 13
1. Everyone has the right to freedom of movement and residence within the borders of each State.
2. Everyone has the right to leave any country, including his own, and to return to his country.

In 1989, Czechoslovakia opened its borders. For the first time since 1948 its citizens were allowed to travel abroad freely, as stated in Article 13 (2) of the UDHR.

'the right to freedom of movement

Article 14
1. Everyone has the right to seek and to enjoy in other countries asylum from persecution.
2. This right may not be invoked in the case of prosecutions genuinely arising from non-political crimes or from acts contrary to the purposes and principles of the United Nations.

Article 15
1. Everyone has the right to a nationality.
2. No one shall be arbitrarily deprived of his nationality nor denied the right to change his nationality.

Freedom to move about is a valued right; taking freedom away is considered a harsh punishment by many societies.

NATIONALITY AND IMMIGRATION

Date: 1993-1995
Place: Cambodia
The issue: Depriving people of their nationality

In early 1993, more than 30,000 people fled their homes in Cambodia, escaping across the border to neighbouring Vietnam. They were fleeing the long-running civil conflict between government forces and an extreme Communist opposition group, the Khmer Rouge. Those who had fled were from a community who had lived in central Cambodia for generations. Although they were of Vietnamese ethnic origin, they spoke the Cambodian language, Khmer, and considered themselves to be Cambodian.

By 1995, many of those who had fled the fighting wanted to return home, but the Cambodian government refused to recognize them as Cambodian citizens. It would not allow them back into Cambodia and they became stateless. They lost their homes and could not return to their villages.

(Above) A rare picture of the Khmer Rouge leader, Pol Pot, in Western Cambodia. It is believed to have been taken in 1989.

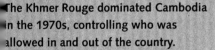

The Khmer Rouge dominated Cambodia in the 1970s, controlling who was allowed in and out of the country.

In Cambodia, fighting between the Khmer Rouge and other forces produced many refugee crises.

Even though Article 15 of the Universal Declaration of Human Rights encourages governments to honour nationality, the Cambodian government passed a law deciding who was a Cambodian citizen, excluding some people who previously had held Cambodian nationality.

What is nationality?

Article 15 of the UDHR upholds everyone's right to nationality. Nationality is your right to be a citizen of a country on the grounds of your origin, your birth or through naturalization, where someone originally from one country becomes a legal citizen of another. In a practical sense, it gives people a geographical location, a place on a map where they come from. It also means that someone from that location is entitled to the protection of the laws in that country.

'a sense of belonging'

But nationality is more than that: it gives people a sense of belonging, it is an important part of someone's identity. To take away an individual's or a group's nationality, as happened in Cambodia, is to deny a fundamental right.

Nationality and persecution

Since the Second World War, despite the UDHR, many minority groups have faced persecution in the countries in which they were born. Minorities within a country can develop when groups of enterprising people leave their country of origin for opportunities abroad. Chinese and Indian people have settled in South-East Asia and Africa, for example, in the hope of achieving a better lifestyle. The fact that these minorities seem to do well in business can lead to resentment from the established community, and, in some instances, this can lead to persecution of the new group.

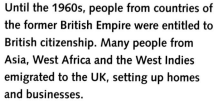

Until the 1960s, people from countries of the former British Empire were entitled to British citizenship. Many people from Asia, West Africa and the West Indies emigrated to the UK, setting up homes and businesses.

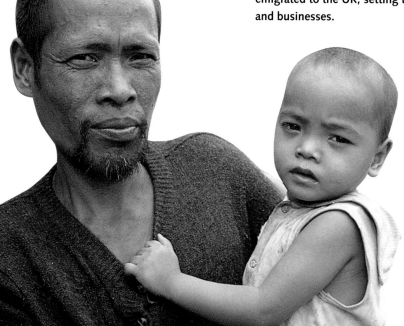

(Right) For a child, losing your home is more unsettling than losing your nationality. But for these Cambodian refugees, they lost their homes because they lost their nationality.

In Uganda in the 1950s and 1960s people of Asian ethnic origin controlled many businesses. In 1971, the military ruler of Uganda, General Idi Amin, decided that they had to leave the country and ordered tens of thousands of Asians to leave because they were not Ugandan citizens.

Depriving people of their nationality and homes creates much resentment and confusion. It also disrupts relations between countries because solutions as to where these people should go need to be found. Many of the Asian population from India held British passports, from the days when Uganda was a British colony. Britain was looked on as being responsible for solving the problem. But Britain did not welcome the Ugandan Asians until international pressure led to a change of policy.

Nationality and a sense of identity

The issue of nationality became very important in 1918 at the end of the First World War when a number of small countries were created following the break-up of two multi-national states, the Austro-Hungarian and the Ottoman empires. The new nations were not always united

(Above) Between 1971-1978, President Idi Amin's forces killed 300,000 Ugandans including Acholi and Lango peoples.

by being made up of one people, one religion or one language. Many people felt they could not stay in the places where they were born because they would be in a minority. Different groups fought for power in the newly created states. There were massacres of peoples, including Assyrians, Armenians, Chaldeans, Jews, Turks, Serbs and Macedonians.

(Below) The Austro-Hungarian and Ottoman Empires prior to 1918 and the new borders after this date.

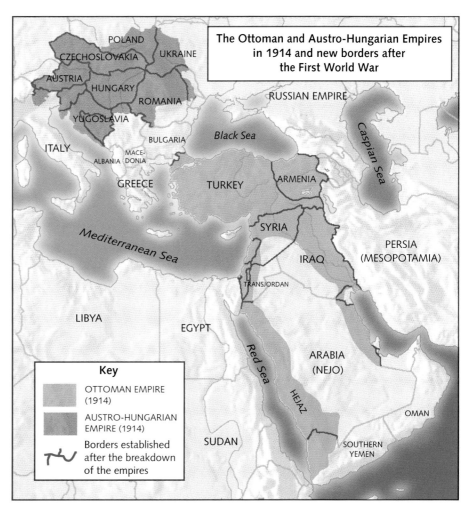

The Ottoman and Austro-Hungarian Empires in 1914 and new borders after the First World War

POLAND
CZECHOSLOVAKIA   UKRAINE
AUSTRIA
HUNGARY
ROMANIA   RUSSIAN EMPIRE
YUGOSLAVIA
ITALY   BULGARIA   *Black Sea*
          MACE-
ALBANIA DONIA
GREECE   TURKEY   ARMENIA
                                          Caspian Sea
Mediterranean Sea   SYRIA
                                          PERSIA
                                    IRAQ (MESOPOTAMIA)
TRANSJORDAN
LIBYA   EGYPT
                        Red Sea   ARABIA
                                          (NEJO)
Key   HEJAZ
OTTOMAN EMPIRE   OMAN
(1914)
AUSTRO-HUNGARIAN
EMPIRE (1914)   SUDAN   SOUTHERN
Borders established   YEMEN
after the breakdown
of the empires

Fridtjof Nansen (left) was a Norwegian explorer who was appointed by the League of Nations to find a solution to the refugee problem in 1921. He believed that the best solution was that they should be able to return home, but he realized that this was not always possible. Those who were made stateless needed papers to enable them to travel, and he devised the Nansen passport (above) to help them in their plight.

Nations and immigration controls

Before the late nineteenth century people were able to travel freely throughout the world. Between 1820 and 1930 over 70 million Europeans left their homelands to travel to the United States, South America and Australia. They hoped they would find a better lifestyle in these developing countries where there was more land and work. This process is known as emigration, when people travel from one country to settle in another.

These massive upheavals in people's lives produced nearly two million refugees fleeing the massacres. They left their homes and had no papers to say who they were. Today, nationality entitles people to a passport from their home country, which allows them to travel. But these people did not have a nationality. In 1921 the League of Nations (an earlier version of the United Nations) appointed Fridtjof Nansen to look after the refugee problem. He quickly realized that the refugees needed either help to go home or, if that was not possible, to be given travel documents so they could settle in another country. The so-called 'Nansen passport' was given to the many refugees who were resettled in Europe and Asia. Without the passports they would not have been able to settle at all.

However, the events of the late nineteenth and early twentieth centuries, increasing refugee problems and the concern of governments over the economy (or wealth) of their countries have led many nations to protect themselves from too many new inhabitants by introducing immigration controls. This means controlling the numbers of people allowed to settle in a country by introducing laws and rules.

When a country's economy is poor and there are not enough jobs, its government tends to keep strict controls on those allowed in. Some countries will allow highly skilled people to settle but keep out the unskilled. Other countries may need unskilled people to do the jobs that no one in the country wants to do, so the immigration controls are relaxed to attract people willing to do the work from abroad.

'**governments tend to keep strict controls**'

Between 1942 and 1945, 220,000 contract labourers were temporarily allowed to work in the United States. Many came from across the Mexican border.

In Ireland the failure of the potato crop in 1846 left many people without food or a livelihood; thousands emigrated to England and the United States.

For example, the 1902 Aliens Act restricted the number of Jewish immigrants allowed into Britain from Eastern Europe. However, after the Second World War ended in 1945, Britain needed people to help rebuild the country so it opened its doors to people from former British colonies, including India and the Caribbean. Similarly, the US had passed laws in 1882 to limit the number of Asian immigrants seeking work there. After the Second World War it, too, needed people to develop its economy. Contract labourers were brought in from Mexico.

15

Asian women in the UK today can still experience difficulties in arranging for their foreign-born husbands to join them.

Immigration and splitting families

Article 16 of the Universal Declaration of Human Rights upholds a person's right to marry whom they choose. In theory this means that anyone who marries a foreign national should be entitled to be joined by their wife or husband. This was raised as an issue after the Second World War when 125,000 war brides from European and other countries were allowed to join their husbands in the United States. However, then as now, it was not an automatic right.

Date:
2004
Place:
United States of America
Issue:
The effect of immigration controls on people's lives

Daniella Sava, 29, and her sister Vicki, 25, who emigrated to the USA in 1991, returned to their native Romania in 2002 to marry in a double civil ceremony. In March 2003, the sisters, who are naturalized Americans, filed immigration papers for their husbands, asking for temporary visas. The sisters live with their mother there and both hold down two jobs.

By 2004, however, their husbands still had not joined them. A US consular officer in Romania was suspicious because the sisters had had short relationships with their future husbands. The officer believed they married for money instead of love. But the sisters are continuing their efforts to be reunited with their husbands. 'They keep saying when you're an American citizen, you have all the rights like any other American,' Daniella said. 'For us, it's a completely different story.'

'separated from their husbands'

Countries often overlook these rights in their determination to control immigration. Some countries discriminate against women by not allowing husbands to enter because they will take jobs at a time of unemployment. Husbands are more likely to be allowed to have their wives join them because it is assumed that they will support their wives. Britain's immigration rules state that a wife or husband can only join their partner if it is shown that they will be able to live without assistance from the state in providing income support or housing. This means that wealthy people who have jobs are more likely to succeed in their applications to have their wife or husband join them.

(Left) Many US service men married European women during the Second World War.

Turkish demonstrators in Germany. Children of Turkish migrant parents, even if born in Germany, are not given automatic citizenship.

Building a nation state

Not all countries are against immigration. Some countries encourage certain people to come and settle. They may want to encourage highly skilled people who will help build up the country's economy, or wealth, by providing services that the country needs. Some governments, such as those of Germany or Israel, have encouraged the resettlement in their countries of those whom they regard as their people in other parts of the world.

Many people of German origin who had been living in countries outside Germany, sometimes for generations, were encouraged to resettle within the country's borders. Between 1988 and 1993, about 1.4 million Germans from Poland, Romania and parts of the Soviet Union were welcomed into the country. However, Germany only welcomed Germans. Many Turks lived in Germany as temporary workers but were never offered nationality or the right to have their families join them. Eventually, under pressure, Germany changed its laws so that those Turks who had lived in Germany for a long time were allowed to have German nationality.

17

FREEDOM OF MOVEMENT

Date: 1961
Place: Berlin, Germany
Issue: Curbing people's freedom to travel

In 1945, at the end of the Second World War, Germany was occupied by the victorious armies of the Soviet Union, the United States, Britain and France and the country was divided between them. The capital of Germany, Berlin, was also divided into four parts and occupied by each army. The Eastern parts of Germany, occupied by Soviet troops, became the German Democratic Republic, a Communist country; the Western parts, occupied by the armies of France, Britain and the US, became the Federal Republic of Germany. However, people were still able to come and go freely across the border dividing the two countries.

It soon became clear, though, that people were leaving East Germany for West Germany where there was more freedom. In 1961, in order to stem the tide of people leaving, the East Germans hurriedly built a barbed-wire fence and then a high concrete wall along the border crossing Berlin. Train services between the two parts of the city were stopped and East German commuters with jobs in West Germany were turned back. The wall remained in place for 28 years until people brought it down in 1989 when the Communists lost their hold on power.

In an effort to live a freer life under democratic rule, many people died trying to escape over the wall, but there were also some spectacular escapes.

East German soldiers attach additional barbed wire to the border between the Eastern sector and the Western sector of Berlin, on 21 August 1961. The fencing was quickly replaced with a concrete wall, with checkpoint towers and sentries.

Communism is a set of ideas about how people should own and control the land, work and wealth of their country through the state. It was supposed to lead to a more equal society, in which wealth would be distributed more fairly. In practice, this has not always proved to be the case.

Many countries protect their borders with guarded checkpoints. Most governments are anxious to know why

'supposed to lead to a more equal society'

visitors are entering their country, and checking travel documents at borders is one way to monitor this. But as with East Berlin, some Communist countries have been much stricter about who is allowed to come and go.

(Left) In June 1989, a student protest in support of human rights was attacked by Chinese troops in Tiananmen Square in Beijing. The Communist government will not accept any protests against its policies.

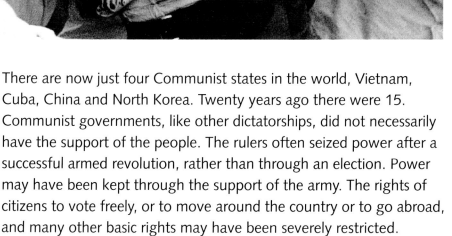

The collapse of Communism in the former Soviet Union has produced much fighting and chaos. Many internal borders, such as this one between Abkhazia and the rest of Georgia, are patrolled at all times.

There are now just four Communist states in the world, Vietnam, Cuba, China and North Korea. Twenty years ago there were 15. Communist governments, like other dictatorships, did not necessarily have the support of the people. The rulers often seized power after a successful armed revolution, rather than through an election. Power may have been kept through the support of the army. The rights of citizens to vote freely, or to move around the country or to go abroad, and many other basic rights may have been severely restricted.

Public criticism

The reason for this was that the governments of these countries did not want opposition groups to organize and challenge their power. Nor did they want to lose the most gifted people, who were needed to build up the strength and economy of the country but who might be tempted to seek a freer lifestyle elsewhere. Consequently, only chosen groups of citizens were given permission to travel abroad – these included diplomats, athletes and performers. Occasionally some of these people would publicly criticize Communism when they left their country – and would refuse to return home.

East Timor, once a colony of Portugal, was taken over by the Indonesian army in 1975. In the period after the invasion, some 100,000 Timorese people, a sixth of the population, are estimated to

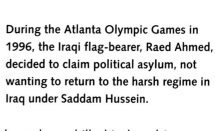

During the Atlanta Olympic Games in 1996, the Iraqi flag-bearer, Raed Ahmed, decided to claim political asylum, not wanting to return to the harsh regime in Iraq under Saddam Hussein.

have been killed in bombing or shooting by the Indonesian Army or to have died from starvation due to the effects of war. In 1999, the Timorese people voted overwhelmingly for independence. Because of this, pro-Indonesian militia gangs terrorized the population before an international peacekeeping force arrived. A UN administration was put in place in 1999, and elections were held in 2001. East Timor became independent on 20 May 2002.

The Indonesian government did not like to be criticized about its policies on East Timor. This demonstration was set up to demand that the International Committee for the Red Cross (ICRC) should not 'interfere' in Timorese issues.

Restrictions on movement

The violation of human rights does take place in democracies as well as under dictatorships. But it is generally accepted that individuals have more freedom under a democratic system. Every country places certain restrictions on its people, however. Many nations conduct military exercises or scientific experiments on special sites and so forbid people from going onto that land.

Living in a democracy

In a democratic country, all citizens are entitled to have a say in how the country is run. This is achieved by each person over a certain age being able to vote for someone to represent their community, usually in a parliament. In a democracy, if people do not like the way the country is being run they can, after a few years, vote for a different representative, and possibly a different government. If a government does not seem to be upholding basic human rights and freedoms the people can put pressure on the government to take notice of these rights by threatening not to vote them into power at the next election.

In democracies, elections are held at frequent intervals allowing the people to decide which party they want as their government.

Even democracies restrict the movement of people. France uses an atoll in the Pacific Ocean, Mururoa, to test its nuclear bombs. This caused huge protests; Greenpeace activists tried to stop the tests, but were arrested for entering the 'no entry' zone set around the island.

Further still, the governments of some democratic countries will not allow their citizens to visit countries they do not approve of. For example, the United States will not allow tourists to go to the island of Cuba because it does not approve of Cuba's Communist government.

Date:
1995
Place:
Belgium
Issue:

The right to work in another European Union country

Jean-Marc Bosman was a footballer whose two-year contract with Liege Football Club had run out. He was offered a new contract but was not happy with the rate of pay. He arranged a transfer to a French club but Liege FC asked for a very high transfer fee and the move fell through. Bosman took his case to the European Court of Justice. He argued that the transfer fee was a form of illegal bondage because it tied him to the club and interfered with his freedom of movement. The Court agreed and ruled that footballers who no longer had contracts should be able to move to other European clubs without any transfer fees being paid.

It took Jean-Marc Bosman many years to win his case before the European Court of Justice. His victory came too late for him to resume his career but it has allowed many talented footballers to move freely to overseas clubs at the end of their contracts.

Freedom to work in other countries

The United States and European countries place obstacles in the way of people wishing to enter their countries to come and work. The United States has a quota system that has become more restrictive since the terrorism of 11 September 2001. In many European countries job applicants have to apply for a work permit before they can take up the job. They will get a work permit if they can show that they are better suited to the job than people who are already settled in the country.

'Some restrictions are gradually changing'

In some parts of the world restrictions on travel are changing to allow greater mobility. Article 48 of the Treaty of Rome, which established the European Union (EU) in 1957, guarantees freedom of movement to the workers of the member states across national frontiers. This means that those living within the EU, like Jean-Marc Bosman, can move to work in other EU countries and bring their families with them.

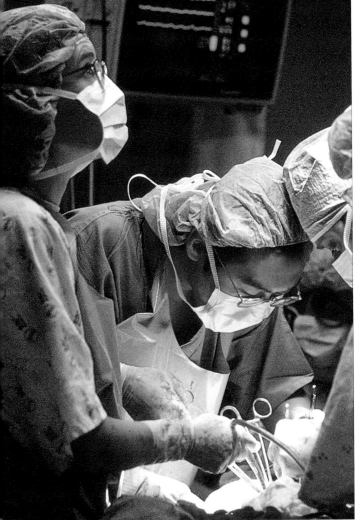

Additionally, it is still easier for people from wealthier backgrounds and countries to move from one country to another. For poorer people, the possibilities are more limited. Firstly, if you are poor it is far harder to afford the transport to travel between countries. Secondly, countries are reluctant to accept people to settle there if they feel that the newcomers will drain the country's resources, instead of contributing to them. However, there are some instances when governments do allow people from whole communities to cross their borders.

(Above) The skills of surgeons are in demand all round the world. Their work often allows them to settle in countries of their choice.

(Right) Modes of travelling vary according to where you live and what you can afford.

Desired professions

Despite these changes, it is still very much easier for people in desired professions, such as doctors or engineers, to gain access to jobs abroad. These are people who are wanted by all countries, both industrialized and developing, to help keep the country going, or to help develop the country further.

Date: 1994
Place: Rwanda, Africa
Issue: Becoming a refugee

In the small densely-populated central African country of Rwanda, there had been a long-running conflict between the Tutsi minority, who used to rule the country, and the Hutu majority. Many Tutsis had fled Rwanda after the Hutu uprising in 1959.

Some form of control was maintained until April 1994 when the presidents of Rwanda and neighbouring Burundi were killed when their plane was shot down. In Rwanda, a well-planned massacre by trained Hutu military followed. Some 500,000 people were killed, mainly Tutsis but also Hutus who were thought to be Tutsi supporters. Panic set in and over a million Rwandans sought refuge in Zaire, Tanzania and other neighbouring countries.

The Tutsis fled fearing the continued persecution and killing of their people. The Hutus fled fearing the angry reaction of the Tutsi-led rebel army, the Rwandese Patriotic Front.

Former members of the Hutu government managed to take control of the refugee camps in Zaire and prevented people from returning home. This meant the refugee crisis continued even when the fighting in Rwanda had stopped.

'prevented people from returning home'

Refugee camps are not always places of safety. In Zaire thousands of Rwandan refugees died within days of arriving in Goma camp because there was not enough water for everyone and there was an outbreak of dysentery, a severe form of diarrhoea.

Flooding in Quanzhou City in China resulted in thousands of people having to abandon their homes. Though they are not classed as refugees, because they are not moving because of fear of persecution, they still urgently need shelter and food.

In Africa there are long-term problems of poverty and political instability. Many African countries were seized by European powers, like Great Britain, France, Belgium, Germany, Portugal and Italy, during the nineteenth century. They were run as colonies until they gained independence between 1958 and 1975. Since independence, many of the African countries have found it difficult to maintain economic and political stability. There have been many military take-overs and civil wars which have caused huge refugee crises and starvation in Ethiopia, Mozambique, Somalia, Burundi and many other countries. The wars have made it difficult for such countries to develop and to cope with the issue of poverty.

What causes movement of peoples?

Some people flee their homes and their countries because they are being persecuted by their government. Others flee because there is fighting in their country and they are afraid that soldiers will kill them. These people are officially described as refugees. Others may be forced to leave their homes because of a large-scale disaster, such as floods. Though they are not fleeing persecution, and so are not classed as refugees, whole communities can still be forced to move.

Those who flee to other countries may be offered shelter, often in camps, and rations to ensure they have enough to eat. Article 14 of the Universal Declaration of Human Rights upholds the right of asylum for those who are fleeing persecution. When the refugee crisis is on a massive scale, the international community may try to help solve the problem. People who lose everything by becoming refugees need assistance; to leave them in need would be to deny them their human rights.

Fighting in Chechnya between Russian forces and those in favour of an independent Chechnya led to major refugee crises in neighbouring areas.

Refugees and 'internally displaced people' (people who have to leave their homes, but remain within their own country) are among the biggest human rights problems facing the world today. Many countries are involved with refugees, either by causing people to flee or by receiving refugees, or both. Across the world in 2002, there were 20.6 million refugees and internally displaced people – about one out of every 300 people on earth.

A growing problem

At the end of the Second World War some 30 million people were homeless as a result of the worldwide fighting. About 12 million Germans were expelled from areas of Eastern Europe occupied by Soviet troops. The United Nations set up various organizations to deal with the problem. In 1951, the UN agreed the International Convention on the Status of Refugees. It defined the term refugee as anyone who leaves a country and is unable or unwilling to return to it because of a 'well-founded fear of persecution'.

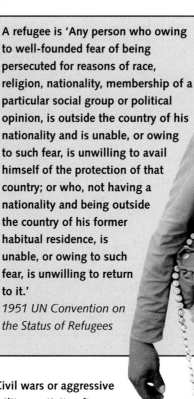

A refugee is 'Any person who owing to well-founded fear of being persecuted for reasons of race, religion, nationality, membership of a particular social group or political opinion, is outside the country of his nationality and is unable, or owing to such fear, is unwilling to avail himself of the protection of that country; or who, not having a nationality and being outside the country of his former habitual residence, is unable, or owing to such fear, is unwilling to return to it.'
1951 UN Convention on the Status of Refugees

Civil wars or aggressive military activity often cause people to feel fearful for their lives.

Date: 2004
Place: United Kingdom
Issue: Asylum for people fleeing civil war

Adam and his family are victims of the civil war in Sudan. His older brother was forced to fight and was killed, so Adam left school to work in his parents' shop. Then in 2003, when Adam was 22, his family's home in Darfur was attacked by government troops who killed his younger sister before arresting him and his father. Adam was tortured and lost the hearing in one ear. He escaped from prison and found his way to a boat in Port Sudan. He expected to travel to America but it landed in the UK in January 2004. Given asylum, Adam now wants to find his father, mother and sister, whom he believes might be in refugee camps.

'Adam was tortured'

Adam's story is one of many recorded by the Refugee Week partnership in their June 2004 report, *Fleeing the Fighting*. More than 70 conflicts were taking place in 52 countries. The UK Home Office noted that 49,370 people applied for asylum in 2003 in the UK, not counting their dependents. Of this total, 74 per cent, or 36,595 applicants, were from countries experiencing civil war.

Some people flee at the outbreak of trouble, others do not want to leave their homes. However, as fighting intensifies many people are left with no option and have to leave.

27

Asylum

The idea of asylum (seeking a safe place to stay) is found throughout history. In the past, refugees were able to travel quite freely to seek shelter in other lands.

Seeking asylum

Traditionally, asylum seekers in Europe were given a lot of help to settle. They were given money, language lessons and sometimes specialized housing. By the later part of the twentieth century the governments of industrialized countries made it more and more difficult for refugees to enter their countries and gain political asylum. Today, most of the world's refugees are from Africa and Asia. They often face a bleak life in camps awaiting their return home as they are not welcome in the countries to which they flee, which have their own problems.

28

(Left) Many refugees accepted as asylum seekers are provided with education and skills that will help them to integrate into the society which they have joined.

(Above) Only a small percentage of Asian and African refugees travel the long distances to seek asylum in industrialized countries.

Date: 1975
Place: Vietnam
Issue: Economic migrants

In 1975, after 30 years of conflict, the Vietnam War ended and Vietnam became a united country under a Communist government. This led to 840,000 refugees leaving Vietnam over the next 15 years. Some left for the neighbouring countries of Cambodia and Laos, while others headed for resettlement in the United States and elsewhere. Some left in tiny boats to be picked up at sea and taken to Hong Kong, the Philippines, Indonesia and other countries in South-East Asia. Initially they were considered genuine refugees but by 1989 most refugees from Vietnam were considered to be economic migrants, leaving their country because of the difficult economic conditions, in search of a better life abroad.

left in tiny boats

Political refugees or economic migrants

In the 1970s and 1980s about 80% of those who fled Vietnam across the seas were known as boat people. They were welcomed as refugees and offered settlement all over the world. The remainder spent years in difficult living conditions, usually in camps in their host countries, waiting for their status to be decided.

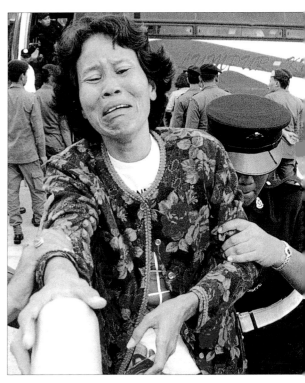

(Above) In April 1996, the Malaysian authorities started to put the 'Orderly Repatriation Programme' into practice. This was an official programme to send its boat people back to Vietnam. Force often had to be used as the refugees were reluctant to return to a country where they had no future.

A distinction was drawn between genuine asylum seekers and economic migrants. In all, 72,000 Vietnamese boat people were returned to their homeland as economic migrants. The remainder refused to go home.

Since the 1980s, many of the industrialized countries have introduced further regulations to try to limit the number of people coming to their shores to seek asylum. They check that those applying for asylum have genuine fears of persecution. The UK and many other countries in the European Union now insist on visitors obtaining visas before they are allowed in. Fines have been introduced for airlines and shipping companies who bring in people with no visa or false papers.

A woman washes her clothes in Ho Chi Minh City, Vietnam. After unification in 1975 and the end of years of war, other nations isolated Vietnam and refused to trade or help rebuild the country. This led to great poverty for most of the Vietnamese people.

A better life

In recent years, there has been a steady increase in the number of people coming to Western Europe to seek asylum. Western governments worry that some asylum seekers are trying to escape poverty at home for a better life. These economic migrants have paid large sums to illegal organizations that smuggle them into Europe, some coming from as far away as China.

Hardships

Although some people may not legally qualify as refugees, they may still have to face many hardships in their own countries. Many flee their homelands because of a lack of opportunities there, or because of violence.

The tightening of refugee legislation in many of the wealthier countries limits the possibility of people moving from poor countries. And if they do try to cross borders they become illegal immigrants who have few rights under international law.

Origin of major refugee populations in 2002

Country of origin	Main countries of asylum	Number of refugees
Afghanistan	Pakistan, Iran	2,481,000
Burundi	Tanzania, D. R. Congo	574,000
Sudan	Uganda, Ethiopia, D.R. Congo, Kenya, Central African Rep.	505,200
Angola	Zambia, D.R. Congo, Namibia, Congo	433,000
Somalia	Kenya, Yemen, Ethiopia, United Kingdom, USA, Djibouti	429,000
D. Rep. Congo	Tanzania, Congo, Zambia, Burundi	415,000
Iraq	Iran, Germany, Netherlands, Sweden	401,000
Bosnia-Herzegovina	Serbia-Montenegro, USA, Sweden	372,000

Major refugee arrivals during 2002

Origin	Main Countries of Asylum	Total arrivals
Liberia	Sierra Leone, Guinea, Ivory Coast	105,000
D. Rep. Congo	Burundi, Tanzania, Zambia	39,000
Somalia	Yeman, Kenya	24,000
Ivory Coast	Liberia, Guinea	22,000
Nigeria	Cameroon	17,000
Sudan	Uganda, Kenya, Central African Rep.	16,000
Angola	Zambia, D.R. Congo	8,000
Rwanda	Uganda, Tanzania	6,000

These figures are taken from the *State of the World's Refugees* (UNHCR) and are dated September 2003. They do not include more than 4 million Palestinians who are covered by a separate mandate of the UN Relief and Works Agency for Palestine Refugees in the Near East (UNRWA).

Date: 1951
Place: United Nations, New York
Issue: Looking after refugees

Mrs Sadako Ogata of Japan served as High Commissioner for Refugees in 1991 to 2000, overseeing refugee issues throughout the world. Ruud Lubbers replaced her in 2001.

When the United Nations agreed the Convention on Refugees in 1951, it also set up the Office of the United Nations High Commissioner for Refugees (UNHCR). This organization does not help refugees directly but works with governments on the refugees' behalf. Over 120 states have signed the Convention on Refugees.

The UNHCR makes sure that governments are acting within the Convention. It encourages governments to provide places for refugees who need to be resettled, as well as encouraging them to find long-term political solutions to refugee problems.

'provide advice... education and training schemes'

It also works with other aid organizations, which provide advice, arrange education and training schemes, offer health care, set up income-generating projects so that refugees can earn money, as well as providing food and emergency shelter.

Palestine has a long history of conflict. After the Second World War, when the State of Israel was established, over a million Arab Palestinians became refugees creating one of the largest refugee populations in the world. Palestinian refugee camps became permanent settlements. The UNHCR is determined to find long-term solutions to such problems.

The UNHCR's strategies

The UNHCR tries to ensure that the human rights of refugees are protected. It ensures that aid agencies provide physical security while trying to find long-term solutions to the political and military situations that have led to the refugee problem. These solutions include trying to stop people having to leave their homes, working to improve conditions in countries destroyed by war, using peace-keeping forces to try to prevent fighting and looking at the whole problem rather than just looking after refugees. It tries to focus the attention of journalists in industrialized countries on crises which need solutions, in order to bring the plight of refugees to the attention of the world.

The right to remain

One way of dealing with refugee problems has been to find ways to make people feel safe enough to stay at home. In 1991, the UN took action to protect one-and-a-half-million Kurds who had fled their homes in northern Iraq after the end of the Gulf War. After Iraq's defeat by the United Nations' forces, the Kurds feared that the Iraqi leader, Saddam Hussein, would start attacking them. US-led forces created 'safe havens' in northern Iraq so that refugees could return to their homeland under protection. The UNHCR then started work rebuilding destroyed villages to provide shelter, while other agencies supplied food and equipment.

After the second Gulf War in 2003, tens of thousands of Kurds returned to lands and cities in Iraq they had lived in, such as the oil-rich city of Kirkuk. Their right to return is outlined in Article 13 of the Universal Declaration of Human Rights.

An Iraqi Kurd, fleeing the fighting in Kurdish territory in northern Iraq, carries his possessions and food to the Turkish border.

A Guatemalan refugee in a camp in Chiapas State in Mexico looks after seedling trees. The UNHCR has run successful training programmes all over the world to help returning refugees.

Emiliano Ramirez was a refugee from Guatemala's long civil war that claimed some 200,000 lives. He was among about 150,000 Guatemalans who fled into Mexico in the early 1980s. By 2001, with peace in their homeland well established, more than 40,000 returned to plots of land given by the Guatemalan government. But many returned to poverty, since their poor country could afford little.

'We spent 15 years in Mexico and returned to poverty'

Four aid organizations, including the UNHCR, helped provide wooden huts for his community of some 150 former refugee families. 'We spent 15 years in Mexico,' said Emiliano, 'and returned to poverty.' But the future looks more hopeful because a peasant cooperative has pooled resources to improve conditions.

The right to return

Many refugees would like to return home once they can be sure they will be safe. Some return when there is no longer any fighting in their home town even though their country remains at war. However, sometimes they return home because it is no longer safe to remain in the host country.

'Many refugees expect to return'

The UNHCR has supervised several programmes to assist those returning home to make sure they are safe. It is now drawing up plans to help return the many Iraqi refugees who for years have been fleeing their country's oppressive regime and several wars. In 2004, some 450,000 lived in refugee-like situations in nearby countries, and UNHCR estimates that 50% to 60% will return, about 240,000 people. It hopes to direct organized returns after the dangers in Iraq have passed.

Jeddah in Saudi Arabia is the home to refugees from Ethiopia. Saudi Arabia welcomed 37,000 Iraqi refugees fleeing Saddam Hussein after the first Gulf War in 1991.

Date:
1994
Place:
Tigre
Issue:
Integration or return

From 1962 to 1991, there was war in Ethiopia between the Ethiopian government and the peoples of Tigre and Eritrea, who wanted to be independent. During this period thousands of children left Eritrea as their families feared they would either be killed or forced to join the Ethiopian army.

In 1986 a Tigrean boy, Ahmed (aged 11), was sent by his family to live with his brother in Sudan.

His father was killed in the fighting and his mother left Eritrea and went to Saudi Arabia to find work as a maid. After two years, his mother was able to send for him to join her in Jeddah. Saudi Arabia is a Muslim country and Ahmed was Muslim but Saudi Arabia is very different from Ethiopia. Ahmed went to a school where they spoke a different kind of Arabic from his own. He found it difficult to make friends and, although he had his mother and brothers, he never got used to living there. After the war in Tigre ended in 1991, he went home to join his grandparents. Ahmed had not been able to settle in Saudi Arabia and although life in Tigre was difficult after the war, it was his home.

Returning home

Returning home can be very difficult emotionally as well as practically. Villages and homes may have been destroyed and need rebuilding. Families have been broken up. Life will not be as it was before and people may find it difficult to live with the memories of their experiences as refugees and victims of war.

The UNHCR has worked on development programmes to help people support themselves once they return. This involves distributing tools and seeds so that people can grow their own food. The UNHCR has also run Quick Impact Projects to provide instant benefits. These have included equipping a fishing co-operative, establishing school libraries, providing training courses, establishing a handicraft centre for women, digging wells and other activities.

Finding solutions to the world's refugee problem is not easy. Peace, prosperity and stability are the essential ingredients. Only if countries work together to achieve these aims, will the massive displacement of peoples stop recurring.

'finding solutions to the world's refugee problems'

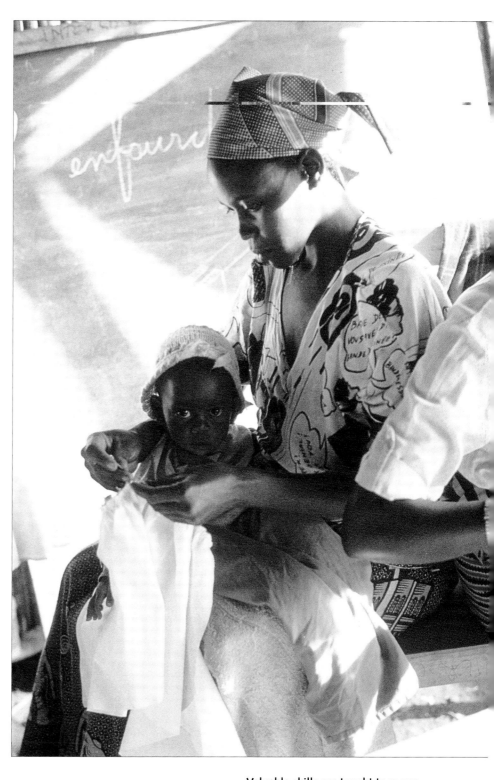

Valuable skills are taught to many refugees in order for them to be able to rebuild their lives on their return home.

Date: 1994
Place: Beijing Intermediate People's Court, China
Issue: A fair trial

In China the government often imprisons its political opponents, using the legal system to find them guilty. They are often charged with vague offences and not allowed to choose a lawyer. Witnesses called against them are not always cross-examined to see if they are telling the truth. But Article 10 of the Universal Declaration of Human Rights states that everyone is entitled to a fair and public hearing by an independent tribunal, or court. Article 11 of the UDHR goes further and states that at a trial all those involved have to assume the accused is innocent until the charges have been proven.

'innocent until charges proven'

In Austin, Texas, USA, a District Court judge is sworn in. In civil cases, judges listen to both sides and then make a judgement. In criminal cases, the judge advises the jury on the law and the jury decides on innocence or guilt.

Gao Yu, a Hong Kong journalist, wrote four articles for two Hong Kong papers reporting on Chinese economic issues from China. She was arrested by the Chinese authorities on 2 October 1993 and charged with revealing important state secrets. She was tried three times in 1994. Each time, the court found that the evidence needed to be checked. She was not released, but kept in detention until the next trial. At her last trial in November 1994 neither she, nor her husband, nor her lawyer were given any notice that the trial was about to take place. The trial was held in secret. She was found guilty and sentenced to six years in jail. She was released in 1999.

Gao Yu did not have a chance to defend herself properly at the trial. Chinese laws on state secrets are vague and are used to catch political opponents of the government.

A fair trial means that all the evidence against the accused will be examined carefully. The accused is able to choose a lawyer, or can represent him or herself. The evidence will be listened to by either a judge or jury, made up of citizens, who then decide the person's innocence or guilt. Most countries have a system of justice designed to ensure that this happens. The UDHR is there to ensure every country follows this system.

Going to prison

Most people agree that taking away someone's freedom is a harsh penalty. Those found guilty of interfering with other people's human rights, by using violence against them or stealing their property for example, have to pay the price of losing their freedom of movement by being sent to jail.

(Below) The price of committing a crime is often imprisonment. With the loss of freedom many other rights that are often taken for granted are also denied.

(Above) Gerry Conlon, one of the Guildford Four, celebrates his freedom after being released from prison in October 1989.

Miscarriage of justice

In any country, however, people who have not necessarily committed any crimes can be found guilty by mistake. Even in democratic countries, where the criminal justice system is supposed to be fair, there are failures and innocent people are sentenced for crimes they did not commit. One of the most famous examples was the case of the Guildford Four in the United Kingdom.

'found guilty by mistake'

In 1974, explosions in the town of Guildford destroyed several buildings and killed 7 people. The terrorist organization, the Irish Republican Army (IRA), claimed responsibility. The police were under pressure to find those who planted the bombs. They arrested many people and eventually four people were charged and tried. They were found guilty and sent to prison. They spent more than 15 years protesting their innocence. Finally the senior judges admitted that many mistakes had been made in presenting the evidence at the trial. The four people were freed in 1989.

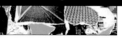

In non-democratic countries abuses of the legal system are more routine. In the Soviet Union, those who did not agree with the Communist regime would be arrested and sent to work camps known as gulags. Unfair trials, leading to the imprisonment of people such as Gao Yu in China, were still not uncommon in the early 21st century. In many countries the government imprisons people simply because they are politically opposed to the government's ideas.

Children in Palestine play 'Intifada' marking the Palestinian uprising against the Israelis in 1987. Israeli officials arrested many Arab children, fearing they were carrying information. They were held in prison without warning for many days.

Members of the Tuaregs, from Algeria, often use maids. The children of maids may find that they are bound as servants too.

Modern forms of slavery

Some people lose their freedom not because the State takes it away from them but because other people do. This can occur when people captured in war are sold into slavery or when poor parents sell their children to serve others in order to raise some extra money. In other instances, parents may not have any control over what happens to their children. For example, Nomadic peoples, such as the Tuaregs, keep women as maids and the maids' children are tied to the family. They can be sold to other families and are expected to do all household work for their new masters. And though this might mean that the children are not free to travel with their mothers, there is nothing the mothers can do about it.

Some workers are similarly tied to their employers in what is known as debt bondage. A parent can pay off a debt by sending a child to work for the person to whom they owe money or an adult can sell himself to settle a debt. Girls and women are sometimes sold by their families into prostitution. It is very difficult for them to escape as they are usually a long way from home and their families will not have them back.

'debt bondage'

Slaves and people in debt bondage have lost their freedom in the sense that although they can go about their daily lives, they are bound to their owners. If they escape, they can be traced and forced to return. Their owners have the money and influence to keep them in a state of fear and dependency. Their freedom to move has been taken away as effectively as if they were locked up.

The Anti-Slavery Society, founded in 1823, is one of the world's oldest human rights organizations. It tries to get rid of these forms of modern slavery, collecting information on abuses and working with governments to try to change laws.

Debt bondage still occurs in India today. Poverty-stricken families sometimes feel they have no choice but to sell their children into service, effectively taking away their freedom to move.

Although Boston, Massachusetts, in the USA (above right), suffered a recession in the 1990s, job prospects there are still good. Though there are opportunities in Bogota, in Colombia (above left), they are not as plentiful as in the United States.

Date:
1990
Place:
Wellesley,
Massachusetts,
United States
Issue:
Staying on after
a year abroad

Alberto, a 17-year-old Colombian boy, spent a year living with a mother and daughter in Wellesley, a small town near Boston. During this year he had access to computers and rock music, he travelled round the United States and had a lifestyle that was a great deal more comfortable than what he was used to at home in Bogota.

Alberto came from a large family where, although his parents had professional jobs, they did not have enough money to send his sisters to university.

Alberto was lucky in that his parents sent him to the United States. The experience opened his eyes to opportunities he would otherwise not have known about. He decided he did not want to return home and he stayed on in the United States, studying engineering at college. After he graduated he married a US citizen and got a well-paid job with the oil company, Texaco. His years abroad led him to feel he wanted a different life from that of his parents.

'opened his eyes to opportunities'

The importance of travel

People in industrialized countries value their freedom to travel and indeed many take their right to travel for granted. Much can be learnt through visiting other places, in your own country and abroad. However, there are many who are still denied these opportunities because of the lack of funding or owing to the political situation in their country.

International understanding

Voluntary Service Overseas (VSO) sends volunteers abroad to work alongside people in poorer countries. The idea is that the volunteers share their skills and extend their experience. All these organizations are trying to promote international understanding as people from different countries learn about each other.

The Daneford Trust is a small charity in London, in the UK, which sets up 'Young Worker Exchange Programmes' which help young people to gain valuable experience in different countries.

(Below) Raleigh International Expeditions combine acquiring new skills with helping to develop existing community projects.

'share their skills and extend their experiences'

Because travel is regarded as an important part of everyone's education there are many organizations which help people to go abroad. In the US there are programmes so that people from developing countries can study there for a year and make contacts with American organizations. It is thought that this will increase US influence in the developing countries when the individuals return home.

In the UK, there are several organizations which promote exchanges between UK schoolchildren and those from other countries. Raleigh International organizes overseas expeditions for young people. They often combine scientific and community work.

Date: 1994
Place: Nigeria
Issue: Being held without trial, denied family contact and medical treatment

In June 1993 Chief Moshood Abiola won the elections for a new president for Nigeria. The military government was not pleased with the result and cancelled the elections. In June 1994 Chief Abiola declared himself president and the military government arrested him. He was then held without trial.

Chief Abiola was held as a prisoner despite there being court orders to release him on bail. Chief Abiola was unable to organize opposition to the military government and had lost his freedom to move. Many foreign governments asked for his release. President Nelson Mandela of South Africa, who was himself a political prisoner for 27 years, also appealed for his release. Amnesty International includes information on Chief Abiola in its reports on human rights in Nigeria and kept up the pressure on the Nigerian government to release him. Chief Abiola died on 7 July 1998 at the age of 60. This was shortly before he was to be released by the new ruler of Nigeria, General Abdulsalam Abubakar.

During his time in prison in Nigeria, Chief Abiola was denied medical treatment for a back injury, and his family was unable to visit him. As well as freedom of movement, he lost many other human rights during his imprisonment. He died in prison in 1998.

Fundamental freedoms

Freedom of movement is much more than being able to travel abroad. It is a fundamental right. When it is taken away, it means that people cannot live their lives in the way they choose. It can mean that they are living in fear. In the case of Chief Abiola, not only has his freedom been taken away without a legal reason, but the loss of his freedom to move takes away many other basic rights as well.

Respecting human rights

There are other organizations working directly to ensure that human rights are respected throughout the world. Amnesty International works to bring justice to individuals whose human rights have been abused. It is an independent organization which brings together professionals and volunteers. It produces detailed reports on human rights abuses, such as the use of torture, illegal detentions and 'disappearances'.

It also brings to people's attention prisoners of conscience – those who are not being held because of a crime, but who have lost their freedom because of their ideas and beliefs.

Individuals write to the governments involved protesting about the breach of human rights and asking for the release of a prisoner. Many of the Amnesty International prisoners of conscience are ordinary people who have run into difficulties with their government. They include journalists who have published articles criticizing government actions, lawyers trying to trace missing people, performers who have publicly spoken out against their governments.

Amnesty International frequently campaigns against the abuse of human rights across the globe. Such campaigns raise awareness of human rights issues and put pressure on governments to acknowledge their responsibilities.

It is only by working to protect human rights that freedom of movement

'underlies all freedoms'

and other freedoms can be ensured. That is why it is important to do something when a government restricts human rights. Writing a letter can sometimes make a difference.

Freedom of movement underlies all other freedoms. Without it we cannot know about the world around us, either our own country or countries further afield. The first sign of a government interfering with its people's rights is often when it denies them freedom of movement. How can you organize a political organization if you cannot meet other people? Even with computers and the ability to communicate over the Internet, the ability to move around the world remains an important freedom. Once that goes, many of the other freedoms are taken away, too.

Amnesty International: an organization that works world-wide for the protection of human rights. Its aim is to look at particular human rights issues such as prisoners of conscience, political prisoners, the death penalty, torture of detainees and 'disappearances'.

asylum: a place of safety. International law states that everyone has a right to seek safety in another country if he or she is under threat in his or her own country.

civil war: fighting between different groups of people in the same country.

Communism: Communism is based on the writings of Karl Marx. It upholds the view that the state, not private individuals, should control industry and agriculture, in order to create a more equal society where wealth is divided as fairly as possible.

concentration camp: prison and work camps where people were kept and deprived of many of their freedoms and basic human rights, including their freedom of movement. The most notorious camps were those set up under Nazi Germany. Millions of people either died, as a result of the horrific conditions, or were killed.

constitution: the basic rules and customs that state how a country is to be organized and governed.

democracy: a country where the government is elected by the people, involving everyone in how the country is run.

developing countries: those countries which are still developing their industries, including manufacturing goods and farming. They often export their produce and buy manufactured goods from abroad.

displaced person: any person who has been forced to leave their home.

economic migrant: a person who leaves his or her country in search of a higher standard of living.

economy: the wealth and resources of a country, measured in terms of the production and consumption of goods and the trading and value of services.

embassy: the offices of the ambassador, or official representing his or her country in another country.

emigration: the movement of people from their country of origin to settle in another country.

European Union: an economic and political association of certain European countries allowing internal free trade. It also permits workers from member states to move freely across national frontiers.

the Holocaust: the mass murder of 11 million civilians, including six million Jews, in Nazi death camps between 1939 and 1945.

humanitarian: showing respect and kindness towards other people in terms of how they should be treated.

immigration: the movement of people into a country to work and live.

industrialized countries: those countries which have advanced economies, where goods are made and services provided, and in which some people enjoy a high standard of living.

Jew: a follower of Judaism, the world religion founded in the Middle East at least 3000 years ago.

League of Nations: an association of countries and states formed into an international organization in 1919 to try to encourage world peace. It was replaced by the United Nations in 1945.

Muslim: a follower of the Islamic religion, which was founded by the prophet Muhammad in AD 622.

Nazi: a shortened form of National Socialist, the political party founded by Adolf Hitler. The Nazi Party ruled Germany from 1933 until 1945, when Germany was defeated in the Second World War. Nazi politics were similar to fascism, with a centralized government which allows no opposition. In addition, it was also strongly racist, believing that some peoples were superior to others. The Nazis used this belief to justify their anti-Jewish policies.

passport: an official document issued by a government certifying the holder's identity and citizenship. It entitles the holder to travel to and from foreign countries.

persecution: the continued harassment or ill-treatment of someone.

prisoner of conscience: anyone imprisoned not for a crime but for their religious or political beliefs.

Red Cross: an international organization bringing relief to victims of war or natural disasters.

refugee: someone who has fled from his or her country because of war or persecution and has been accepted by the government of another country.

slavery: the condition where people are kept as the property of others, and where they are bound to absolute obedience.

Soviet Union: the state made up of Russia, Ukraine, Belorussia and thirteen other republics which existed from 1917 until 1991. It had a Communist government.

state: a nation that is recognized by other nations and which has borders and a government.

trial: an examination in a law court by a judge and jury to decide an issue, usually the guilt or innocence of a person.

United Nations (UN): the body of independent countries formed after the Second World War and designed to act like a world parliament. The founders of the UN hoped to use it to stop further wars and limit human suffering. All the independent nations of the world were expected to join and to try to attain standards of government set by the UN. The UN is funded by contributions from member countries.

Universal Declaration of Human Rights (UDHR): this sets out the basic rights and freedom that concern all aspects of people's lives, from health and welfare, to rights concerning employment, and the right to a fair trial and political security.

visa: an entry in a person's passport that gives permission to visit another country.

work permit: a document that allows a person (usually a foreigner) the right to work in a country.

World Health Organization (WHO): a UN agency which aims to promote health and to control the spread of disease.

USEFUL ADDRESSES

Amnesty International, UK
99-119 Rosebery Avenue
London
EC1R 4RE
www.amnesty.org.uk

Central Bureau for International Educational and Training
3 Bruntsfield Crescent
Edinburgh EH10 4HD
www.centralbureau.org.uk

Cultural Interchange Service
PO Box 538
61 Church Hill
London N21 1LF
www.touchlondon.co.uk/comdir/searchresults.cfm/vocational%20schools

Raleigh International
27 Parsons Green Lane
London SW6 4HZ
www.raleigh.org.uk

The Refugee Council
3 Bondway
London
SW8 1SJ
www.refugeecouncil.org.uk

UNHCR, UK Office
21st Floor
Millbank Tower
Millbank
London
SW1P 4QP
www.unhcr.org.uk

The Refugee Council of Australia
PO Box 946
Glebe NSW 2037
Australia
www.refugeecouncil.org.au

Australian Red Cross
155 Pelham Street
Carlton VIC 3053
Australia
www.redcross.org.au

Amnesty International, Australia
29 Shepherd Street
Chippendale NSW 2008
Australia
www.amnesty.org.au

INDEX